Fahredin Shehu

ORMUS

Fahredin Shehu

ORMUS

Ormus for the Soul

JustFiction Edition

Imprint

Any brand names and product names mentioned in this book are subject to trademark, brand or patent protection and are trademarks or registered trademarks of their respective holders. The use of brand names, product names, common names, trade names, product descriptions etc. even without a particular marking in this work is in no way to be construed to mean that such names may be regarded as unrestricted in respect of trademark and brand protection legislation and could thus be used by anyone.

Cover image: www.ingimage.com

Publisher:
JustFiction! Edition
is a trademark of
International Book Market Service Ltd., member of OmniScriptum Publishing Group
17 Meldrum Street, Beau Bassin 71504, Mauritius
Printed at: see last page
ISBN: 978-620-0-49555-6

Ormus

for the Soul

poetry selection

by

Fahredin Shehu

November 2020

B.H.

-to Fahredin Shehu-

a quiet evening

new moon

a friendly wind

can a little waterfall

turn into Niagara

and all the mountains and forests

of the planet

here

happening

the modest stream

is becoming

an ocean

as we look

reflecting green branches

embracing small mossy rocks

unpretentious freshness

as if

these were the times

B.H.

Before Humanity

witnessing

the monthly visit of our good old neighbor

a rebirth

of

not only Rahovec

Kosovo

Earth

but Nature

as a scattered whole

with its dynamic tranquility

wondering breaths

are becoming

rivers

the little waterfall

is now poetry

wordfree

with a brand new moon

enjoying clarity

flowing together

Tarık Günersel

Poet, playright, actor and director, Tarık Günersel worked at Istanbul City Theater as a dramaturge. His works include Breaths of Infinity (Sonsuzluk Solukları, a mosaic of poems), and My 300th Birthday Speech (short stories). Becoming (Oluşmak) consists of is a collection of his aphorisms and various ideas from world wisdom. His plays include Billennium, Nero and Agrippina, Sociology of Shit, Threat, and Virtually Yours. He has written four libretti for the composer Selman Ada: Ali Baba&40, Blue Dot, Forbidden Love, and Another Planet. His translations into Turkish include works by Arthur Miller, Samuel Beckett, Vaclav Havel ad Savyon Liebrecht. His presentation of World Poetry Day to PEN International in 1997 led to its adoption by UNESCO. Ex-president of PEN Turkey Center, in Tokyo he was elected to PEN International Board for 2010-12. In 2013 he initiated the Earth Civilization Project with various intellectuals from around the world.

Fahredin Shehu's Aromatic Memories
(Ormus by Fahredin Shehu)

The subtle contextualization of his personal poetry in the chronotope of the Medieval Orient, in the kingdom of Ormus/Hormoz, whose etymology refers to the Zoroastrian deity of Ahura Mazda (Lord of Wisdom) is suggestive of a hypnotic setting. A retrospection of the soul. A metempsychotic encounter with the like-minded, an encounter taken as pure faith, as an outburst of the sacral. A memory led by the invisible hand of the unconscious. A poetic laboratory of synesthesia – mixing senses, scents, sounds, colors, tastes, touches.

Fahredin Shehu's poetry is the very touch of that sensitive cocktail that is his poetic language. A reminiscence of the metaphysical quest for oneself by venturing into religious symbolism. Shehu's memory is not only his own. It has absorbed other people's memories as one's own and vice versa. It seeks a world beyond this world, far from ephemeral differences and divisions.

That is why Shehu's poems are meditative, soothing, and their perfume is discrete. The scent of jasmine comes from other times, not from our garden. Its melancholy is pleasant. The past has its own charm – the more scents, sounds, images, tastes and touches it contains, the more powerful it is. That is why it is a palimpsest. Memory turned into word, into verse, into poetry.

Katica Kulavkova, Academic, PhD in Comparative Literature-Sorbonne, Poet, Vice-President PEN Global, Skopje, Macedonia

Petrichor

Earth smell after the rain

a splendid Petrichor brings

Aeons back to life/ to my life

brings a primordial vigor

for eternity and a day more

Just a slide of the past

Out of those petty memoires

the muslin of experiences

unfolded, fluttering on

the light wind one could

believe

is a zephyr that

brought

all aromas

of tinny linden

flowers from afar

It is as we all forgot

the bloodshed caused

by human

depositing suffer

preserving it

for another age

…and the day will come

for ne to stand firm

while the dark wind couldn't

bring down my extremities of gold

I am sure you've heard the story

Of immoral queen and

an immaculate who brought for

a man. A mercy for

the Mankind- confused men

among all…

and all we need is

awareness and let the singers

sing and get the praise

Aromas of the past

Summer nights

and the full moon

on the balcony we enjoyed

herb tea and I can still

hear the knocking

of the metallic spoon

on the bottom of

the porcelain mug

mixing honey- stirring with the tea

a firefly landed

on my arm

the right arm with the thrilled

skin, goose bombs and erected hair

I didn't believe in omens

not even today I read

the dreams with the

vocabulary of Men

Beneath the balcony

huge terracotta amphorae kept

the decaying Iris tuberose

in their sixth year

one more year- one more Me

closing the glass lids above

amphorae and above them

pots of succulents

They were the days

they were the nights when

the life had the human meaning

Those beautiful seconds of the past

He brought a handful

of Tonka beans for the base

She evaporated all liquids

from the petals of jasmine

and dried pistils of the saffron

I collected the dews, early

in the morning

observed and guessed

which star tonight shall

climb to the sky and

decorate it

darker than the ink it was

in those Times. With what I shall

blur tonight

with what I shall quench

my thirst for knowing

when the dews are dried and

the seconds are counted in vein

Another image of the past

I have forgotten

the touch of wet freshly cut grass

and the thrill which runs

faster than a current

from sole to the top of the head

In this urban desert

we didn't cool our feet

like swans in the pond

but with the compressed

Nitrogen in our sneakers

with the perfect cushioning

This time we shall braid

life differently

so we may latter see how

its curls creates a texture

for another age

Mists of the past

A huge mountain shaded

the emerald field with

the dandelions like stars

in the sky all over

The work produces a sweet

essences- I got the bee

zooming in my even hair

blown by the wind

Pearls of sweat in my forehead

some of them dried, felt, blown

taken far from the eyesight

…and the river nearby

gurgling, taking away

some light

They said to us- there were

the souls of drowned men

now wandering in this

vast green field covered

lightly with the mist

Aromatic memories of the past age

The poppies

even…

made it more beautiful

among the metallic sounds

of golden wheat leaves

on my most beloved July

Oh…that very age

I stood firm to expel

my inner daemons and

wrote the first verses

with the smell of earth

before it decomposed bows

twigs and leaves of ivy

sneaked on the trunk of oak trees.

A splendid petrichor!

Down there… the ravine beyond

my eyesight transported

        all my fears

some demoiselle with metallic

       greenish turquoise bodies

silently copulating to extend

their lives through

their progenies in another season

long plus millennia they shall live

in peace, while we

the Human grind souls

chop hearts and suck the blood of each other

Remnants of another aeon

Turquoise ink I save

to write only about love

and blood letter of mortgage

keeping in the box made of

oak tree wood, copper leafs for its lid

and splash of heavy lacquer above all

Moschus sprinkled on my epitaph of Graphene

light letters inscribed

with green laser states

"herein floats the Soul

of a Light-man – a remnant

of another eon".

The bottle of age

Every time and always

I recall mossy ruins of my

distant past where the soul

wandered.

Aghast by the torments and

ropey desires for the life

yet to become.

Lungs are filled with the odor

of oak moss and time by time

pine resin fragrance and

iodized air of the sea.

The breeze brought on that time

soul's nacre of my memories

and the gurgling whims of youth

I pitied them as I do now all

traders who merchandised

their creed for the mustard seed.

Slowly the bottle of age is getting

Filled by the years I have

 to always remember and take

in other dimensions

layered stripes of memory

leaving behind the places on the brain

like bruises turn to yellow.

Wine Cellar

Open those eyes given to you

and fuse with the universe

if you open only the mind's eyes

you will never see the love in full

Conference of Birds by Attar

Translated by Sholeh Wolpe

…keeps centuries of labor

in Grapeland where many have

passed through as conquerors

as those who only wanted to marry

and as those who wanted

to drink the best wine only

in there through millennia

microorganisms were multiplying

and none of us dare to count them

by number none by their age

when I opened my eyes and fused

my glance with the luminous star

undressing her devoré

I could see her torso and

the fog unfurling from her body

dispersing across the universe

a singularity in its vastness

spell bounded our vision

I could see none but us

There was a cellar- up there

pouring that wine from turquoise

amphora- some said it was ambrosia

that Illyrian sages extracted from

honey and served in Delphi Oracle

some said it was only a water

that dropped us mercy and in it

the particles of Soul and fractals

of the life that has yet to come

Prayer's Rug

With the power of another World

I borrow the moment

where remembrance and longing

are spine like a silk thread

for the Prayer's Rug.

Velvet Notebook

On the aquamarine velvet notebook

a heavy Pen writes harshly

with the blood instead of ink and

the straight letters for the curved world

"V" the sign

...and the flock of pilgrim birds flew

in the distant shores

on the way marking the V sign

in the sky aware of flight and bones

full of air and wings by sins sprinkled feathers

Talking the language of God remembering

the words of God upon their very creation

supporting each other avoiding maladies

of what they left behind

not turning back their heads with one aim

they hit the distance to the next exile

the aim of unification to set

in the next dwelling where prayers

are done utterly in vein

and the longing as bitter morsel

is swallowed to cure

the past lives far from bliss

for who know how many will die

on the way toward the known

by the script inscribed in their genes

Crimson pillar

On a crimson pillar of my pain

a demoiselle lands lightly.

Upon a silent shriek of heart's gate

of mine she stands un- thrilled.

I pity... yet I pity those who see

the only friend the one they see on the mirror

for life is no less than a miracle

and all the rest is past or future

Aquamarine clouds of mystery

everything but a dream

non-dream it wasn't

under the shade of blood color maple leaf.

Inter-hearing

Between layers and epithelium

dimensions have no limit

a belling echo is released

amidst canyons of memoires

my walk there

emits a serious spectrum

visible as never before

We sat for a celestial meal

and an instant nap

the pain was precisely cutting us

a laser from the emerald head which

was extracted from arranged layers of granite

There in Antwerp Masters

the diamond cutters pray

prior to commencing their work

We never pray the Moses prayer Ta Ha 114

What kind of ignoramus we are

there's no tongue knotted and those

unknotted from nine knots that

may say the grandeur and the volume

Political children were listening shrieks

of their pain their dirty toilets

People's malfeasants, merchants of their souls
were mocking the others misfortune and their

fear they were layering deep in their soul to take

away as their solely own dowry

Dark forces wearing shinny accoutrements
blinding thus the easy goers and the poor

I heard every move
each of them releasing a weeping sound
between Knowledge, Destiny, Experience and
slides of Life's occurrences

We observe and we feel bad

we listen between pores of collective memories

we march down the Abyss

reckon the sinking and recall

Erica Yong, Fear from flying

That which in the beginning was LOGOS

it remained so

That which in the beginning was READ!

it remained so

I say HEARKEN!

let it be so

Whereas US shall inter-hear

with the ears of our heart

for Eternity and

a Day more

Let the Human...

Let it be the last leaf

that felt in early spring

in there, in here, in everywhere

when the blooming Acacia

intoxicates with the divine perfume,

that fragrance from the doorsteps

                         of Paradise's Gate

filling chests and dazes hearts

Let the World stand today

celebrating the same loftiness

of our Souls where colors

only enriches the bouquet

of Humanity and rejoice

its abundance making jealous

all other creation- even those

manlike predators that see

no mercy in blood shedding

and bizarre exploitation

Let the Men nowadays

understand the difference

of Man and other Creation

is merely to realize how

beautiful is to be a Human

and that the only suffice

in this plentitude and diversity.

Tapestry of Being

there are two things that

Man strives to understand

Love and Poetry

for they became

the show of the profane

on that very day

when the men shall undress them

make them naked and hear

the cry as of the Newborn

the blast from the sky shall

blind the rest and all clouds

shall restart

there are two things that

can reset time

Love and Poetry

for they became

the heavy slide that time

cannot drop to light

on that very day the rest

shall see the moving images

a dreamlike manifestation

they could hardly believe

until they melt in and become

a part of it

for another aeon

the blast from the heart shall

beam-blow the truth

in a time based tapestry of being

Whom to challenge

On the sky wide dome

clouds were forming the story

he tried to jump

never competing anyone

Himself was his own challenge

three times he competed

and exceeded himself

himself was his in suffice

himself was his counterpart

and it remained so

Integration

Strange but real

sad but true

weird but still enduring

what comes next as unknown

show of an irrational

is this a sealed destiny

or a clay-like life that

I may craft my Galatea and

erase the borders of distinction

and doubt whether it

is Love-Life or Life-Love entity

or both simultaneously happening

leaving me to eternally ponder deeply

what it is or what it may be in my struggle

to make it US for US is a total fulfillment

the integration to the ONE- The Real.

...as it was in the beginning

They gave up all definitions

layered fossils beneath the argue-

who's older hen or the egg

Massive droplets of rain

the soil as dry as talcum

release the petrichor we largely

enjoyed- the one we miss

massively today and more and more

in search of poetics and truth

the road we passed in vein

if it goes out of selves

than nothing have we ever achieved

the World was not ready yet

to absorb a living human

even up between the heavy clouds

the breath is focused on the Constellation

of the heart. Some thousand nerves

from the brain of the heart

which human named it Intuition

we laugh upon every definition

and still none can order

a meal with algorithm

but solely by word

as it was

…in the beginning

Complainers

When organic and synthetic algorithm

merge as nail and flesh and

when men shall choose

who's going to love the Absolute?

no other essence or aldehyde

shall perfume our souls

the complainers will love

heavy tears that hardly leak and

all sorts of balms and collagen

to heal their wounds

neither shame nor pity

no other life's form rather than

Life itself will bring solace

to the indifference once

proclaimed holy

Some strange kind of bliss

Thinner than the air

today I dwell in higher

form of bioenergy- the light in

a front, the light behind

the light up, the light down

the light out, the light in

all smells of pleasure

enfolding his mortal flash

all sounds of serenity

turned with this cosmic sound

all fears disappear

all memoires disappear

all tastes disappear

all whishes disappear too

all I want is bliss

Idyllic winter landscape

Parochial entities in

idyllic winter landscapes

tons of un- heard melodies

spreading a skunk

up and down till

the highness of the white clouds

Whom to pity

whom to mercy beyond

       the imaginable

Whom to lay down

the soul on the palm of hand without lines

no palmistry reader may define

the roadmap of perpetual ignorance

Older than she showed

On that Thursday afternoon

heavy clouds merged with ice flakes

and the heavy rain is about to

blow away not only remnants but

The bows and un-ripe fruits

from the Peach tree

and the rest of the orchard

Even fences that hindered

rosters and hens of a neighbor

to cross the alley of veggies

she took care so ardently

Never she knew the dates but

counted days by eggs and

and the mornings by the rooster alarm

She put four sieves on the four corners

of the house- an old belief to preserve her plants

from a heavy hail

in her hair the happiness and sorrow braided

in her azure blue eyes is the image

in the fractals of the universe

in her heart – a cosmic singularity

in her walk- the graciousness

of a honey-face fairy

…but on that Thursday afternoon

she feared death of many

not her own, No. Because she lived

in her tenth life of circular realization

The Theurgist of Word

Pealing pomegranate while

Winter was approaching and

handful of wall nuts he gave me

to show how much he cared about

the one who wants to become a physician

Then the war started in Croatia and

he got back to learn swimming

in the ocean of the Eastern knowledge

said knowledge as he was far from the Wisdom

He even abandoned drying the leaves

seeds, roots and distilling petals

and the pollen- using honey to heal

his body and the prayers to ease

his restless soul

While he continued to study still

from the Taoist pharmacopeia

a receptive dream became

a vision that appeared

out of every perception:

a building of honeycomb shape

Forty neon white light entities surrounded

him, standing in the middle of a huge hall

A ten tons large book, a written parchment

instead of paper- round letters he could

not read- a brass emptied perfume bottle

in the middle of the giant book as if it

was embraced by the parchment

The perfume filled the vast hall and

a lighted white eye-blinding hand

touched his right shoulder

to wake him up- to awaken him

for some decades to come

…and he left his bed

a wetted by sweat pillow and

mattress of Moschus smell was hardly removed

He opened a window

like a baboon stretched his palms

toward the morning sun

to absorb rays- to fill his spirit

with life and to realize he is

what he is- a Theurgist of Word

No point

Ice chunks floating on the turmoil sea

by standing man full of sorrow recalls

when he was not alone

He wanted to roll a dice of

life and death but with whom

Perhaps with his whims and memories

of the past days when the youth

outburst and the path was not

red with rose petals thrown upon the carpet

nor it ever was a fully thorn thrown

alley of despair

When even water is bitter and

the fragrant extremities of plants

stretched their bio-limbs to touch

the sun rays of the late fall

Chirping voices of the birds somehow

made him think he's experiencing

the last days on this planet of hate

where love had had evaporated

its essence for long plus times

even a tornado now wouldn't

                     surprise him

so for time and time again

if it is not in vain said that:

"When none and nothing

is able to surprise you

what's the point of living and

despite all living without

The Beloved"

Remnants of nowadays

The old saddler in a front of

                     his workshop

braids the smoke of heavy tobacco

in a mildly hot summer day

observing the passengers

with the cellphones and prolonged

noses on it, one may think they

are all Pinocchios- a crafted

liars and deceivers

In an old city quarter, in this very

heart of the past occasions

the pigeons flying over without the fear

there were flies on the decayed

fruit remnants on the pavement

thrown by the careless pupils

in their procession toward the school

A siren of a maddened machine

warned- woke up all

who stood there bewildered

Far from the eyesight much farther from the heart

We used to collect the licorice roots

never realized what she used them for

he was cooking in a huge dish

the maple to prepare syrup

Winter was approaching elegantly

we even felt it in our bones

guess what pain felt my grandmother

Our orchard was not so huge

enough to plant all kind of saplings

and other vegetables- sufficient for those

who don't demand a cent from a neighbor

We never knew what the war stood for

apart from what we saw on the TV

Iran- Iraq war

far from sight- much farther from the heart

She died while I was studying

what other merely dropped a globule

of sweat to go there

Hard were those letters

triple harder were the syntaxes and

Trigon lexicography

not Kabbalah- not the mystical science

of letters and numbers

A language of becoming knowing

of the tenth reincarnation of suffer

Yet today I am a silhouette and

gloomy- bitter dark than the darkest stone

Worry-less

Old wine yard was among few

Orchards my late father cultivated

as I strived art by then

Mother rabbit left the nest

in search for the food. There- small rabbits

frightened by my shade. They felt

I was still eating meat

The July was hot- when the first sort

of grapes starts to ripen. I collected

the grape leaves on the top of the twigs

for my Mom who used to preserve them

for winter days, to roll meatballs and

rice and spices for a decadent meal

in the frozen days of December

This can never be a bygone

only the smell of a delicious dish today

resurrects all scenario of the life

I used to live carelessly and worry-less

A mere passenger

Our small city still keeps in

           It shoulders

all what our forefathers stood for

work, dignity, respect, bravery

Craftsmanship, parchment folios

of genealogy from the times when

        Sun was adorned as god

She walked bare naked feet

in a stone bridge- in a nearby town

full of history

The fortress of old times was

observing and guarding from

the top of the hill

Down the hill a place vendors used

to call it a devil's valley

they claim to have seen fairies

flying in and out of the shrubs

until the devil appears…and the evil

old ladies all in white tunics

laid long hairs covering their faces

Pagan adorning the evil entity

on the night of the St. George

One day glowered with honeysuckle

fragrance and that of Melissa and Lemongrass

I went to the town and saw her in

her Elemental splendor

Bewildered I was till delirium

upon my awaking- seven comets

braided their tails

The planets left their marks on my skin

to map the path

my path

and

the image of Sagittarius constellation

imprinted on my forehead

so the Watchers can read

the hushed story of the earthly

life of a star walker

a passenger of the Bridge

The shine- the shrine

The mind is not a master in

the art of love;

Love can not labor in the brain

Conference of Birds by Attar

Translated by Sholeh Wolpe

Surrounded by the graves of Sufi masters

the main shrine

preserved times of remembrance

dispels the evil and offers the shelter

to the travelers of all kinds

A spring beneath the shade

of a wine Arbor- older than any

known in the region-

some four hundred years

She will cease to give shade and

fruits on the year when the enemy

killed the master while praying

and remembering

The God's most High Name

Another shall replace it-her

today the replacement celebrated

twenty years- we do not adore it

but enjoy the transformable smell

of earth into a lung-filling pollen

of tiny grape flowers

Yet we can labor Love

still

in our hearts

Ambrosia

A world between two ears

to some… and heavy clouds

to others brings only the storm

and a vortex- below the throat

down to the heart a constellation

of Love- to the sublime numbers

that human can't explain

those Octonions that operates

in eight dimensions

What is human for god's sake

for all those years those who believed

descended from Eve who was a woman

who understood the language of snakes

For all those years and all those sage

humble and the gorgeous arrogant

could not explain

…and the river of gold melted

the clouds of gold-dust

making shade to the beloved

children borne out of love

in their ambrosias they drunk

powered ORMUS to prolong life

to awaken and enlighten

in there two Georges and the Jin

invented the misery

The yellows- thousands killed

in one hour two blasts ands

Georges and Jin called

them yellow ants- just to subdue them

This dry day age of mine

They were classifying stones

to decorate the pavement

a mosaic of life

a mosaic for life and beyond

Friends called me to go

swimming in the river

far from home

Father was strict

I dare not to ask him permission

unless I lied to him as I was

going to shop a chain for my pappy

a Yorkshire terrier

he brought from Vojvodina

some days ago

I didn't know how

to put those days in the memory ampules

to preserve them in a velvet box

all nacre and silver decorated

and satin flushing red inside

smelling the oak moss and ambergris

and Tonka perfume of my Mom

in this dry day age of mine

smog an skunk and rotten

fruits suffocate and drown

us down to the ravine

all blood and bones

of the past ages

No less than three worlds

Sometime feelings

slipped through the soul

like e beach sand

through fingers

later blown by the wind

The sun rays use to feed my cells

giving potency to the exhausted limbs

among bushes and briars

between stone plates it woke up

a lizard that was dormant

in the season of cold

They liked us

the snake guarded

the inherited treasure

Far in another sight

an urban part of the town

the crowd quarrels for a morsel

and the malfeasant cries

for the loss of what he got not

We've never been bond

to the gold of the earth

even when

the stardust felt upon

our sanctuary – the roof was

stable

the basement kept us safe

bees safeguarded from

            negative vibes

It was as I lived in two worlds

        simultaneously,

it is not that I now live

        In less than three

Some prints

On that very day

I got some message

it was not a call

not a letter to invite me

on the banquet of the Wise

It was neither the revelation

so I may delude myself and

proclaim to be a prophet

in an age that killed them all

it was in fat the call

to wake up from the men's lethargy

to wake up for another age

in which the alarm is not

a rooster any longer

not a handcrafted timer

made in some Swiss towns

I stood with my pendulum

it was the pen. Pencil and stylus

depends on the plain surface

I wrote those words

to love and print

for some years to come

Poet's lullaby

In an old archive there are some

strange rules of lime stoned parchment

in them the blood- letters with faded colors

arranged to show a real palindrome

titles illuminated- all gold leaves

She unrolled the parchment

to show me my awe

she read my face completely flabbergasted

It was a script from pre- Babylonian times

none could read/ decipher so far

as for me it was a map for another age

some new prophet of algorithm

could read and benefit

all I could do was to get

bewildered and lost in that image

…these label and price tags

attached to the forehead

I could read and those

crowns and scepters Men

use to hide zealously from

the eyes of the envious

I could also see naked eye

despite my dioptric has doubled

                        through age

Those transparent beings

in expensive dresses and suits

who could guess their gender

Those foods with gold leaves on the top

to show prestige while in the other

fifth of the world hunger and war

devastated and turned all

into ashes. What could poet do?

to praise a tyrant in order to survive

or salute ministers of ill doing

and highlight their worst faculties

to burn all scripts and escape life

when life was only a sequence

while he was in love

After the war took all and

the windblown remnants,

roots and the twigs of plants

and

bones, veins and extremities

of animals in remote parts

of the planet- to somehow hide

to somehow rest us from fear

What may a poet do today

instead, rather than mourn

and lament for the age

that was human

that was full of belief

that was with God and

what may a poet do for

        tomorrow

other than guess the future

as a blind seer thus

to ridicule and mock himself

or what the machine can't

calculate and call it Love

other than Love despite being

that much ignored or better said

tortured or in the worst cases

tormented in between two worlds

in between two ages that were never his…

One day when the poet realizes

he shall hold the key of the gate-

        that gate with the silent shriek

passing in a hush

like the walk of the cat in an old rug

…and the gate will open and

show two directions

one that leads to Love

and

another

that leads to death

Careless as the most careless

the one may be,

            he shall walk

in a golden macadam and feel

the coldness of the precious metal

early in the wetted by dew mornings

        of another world

The poet shall sing and put to sleep

all unrest souls and he shall too

laugh madly with the existence

he left behind- with the life

he dropped like

        a peach kernel

behind his shoulders and never…

never turned his head- not by fear

he could become a salt-stone

but

aghast of human

aghast of human life

he used to live ardently

Hot, heat, rain and restlessness

With the tongues we tried

to catch the water molecules from

the dry air- the camels we were not

in those days our skin became

dark and scale- the fish

we were not!

The first huge raindrop I mentioned

felt between the soil furrows

as open as baby graves

that corrugates our entire being

Whom to pity first

and

whom to forgive

As of my silence-

a long long long serenity

the hearing increased by its magnitude

 I could listen the blood in my veins

and the liquid running

up and down my backspin

the current produced in Mitochondria

to charge my molecules

and give birth to love

...and the Love is the sole faculty

my soul possesses

regardless if she's being sprinkled

with the most expensive Ambergris and

       Oudh or

simply

by priceless Divine Petrichor- the breeze

brought from distance

from the lands unpolluted

    by hatred

Ribbons

Black ribbon on the neck

of tortoise is the mark that

one day they paid a tribute

to love- they scarified their lives

and sung the song of life

The red ribbon beneath

the skin of my throat

is the mark that once upon a day

I paid a tribute to love too

I scarified my being and

sung a lullaby to a poet

the one that was unable to mark

his Art on his forehead and

seal his destiny

Rosary

…made from lava stones

made from amber and some

from the sapphire-

blue as her eyes

In my bygones she entered the room

the wings visible only by the eyes

of the one intoxicated in Beauty

that once it was the Jewel in the Crown

of Eternity- with the smile that shook

the pillars of heavenly abode and

dense the loftiness of the Oxygen and

made it a blue lump of curiosity

With the walk

the graciousness of which

bewitched all my "I-s" – so they

assemble in that Temple where

infrasonic prayers and offers

          and sermons

zooming like horrified bees

the labor of which produces

      a sweet essence

with the rosary- huge pearls

of which I now count the blessings

to live among Human permanently

While MEN merchandise even

their souls for a lump of happiness-

that is a grain of sorrow

and

the dew of curse

To name a misery

I wanted to give another name

to the Art which is difficult

that to be and to the malady

that bears no name

I wanted a misery to give

another name but feared

it might deceit the innocent

who may perceive it as bewilderment

I wanted to give another name

to love which is difficult to maintain

and to a longing that drains

the morrow from the aged bones of mine

The difference

Empty shelves in our hearts

emptied by the most merciless of Men

that only resembled the Sapiens

who forgot through millennia

to find a pot and fill it with mercy

To remind those without a spark

of Truth and without that

what we treasure down and below

the visible and twinkling and

pulsating wealth of spirit

every time they look at the nature

they don't see an endowment

every time we dwell in nature

we unite with every particle

of her touching the erotic zones and

distill the beauty through

her majesty- depollute

what the careless left as corpse

of their siblings they hated most

Bird shades

Shades of birds flying over our heads

they shall die on day- we shall die

too but life has to say something

very important, in a hush it said:

from the day when stones and waters

heard our first cry- chasing love

from afar- out of body that emanates

old and new currents,

 instead

of delivering it from within and

radiate until it burns the feathers

of the crows that brought misfortune

The ill doing of those birds was

unintentional- a program of their

Bio-algorithm. But the malady

is ours to handle as a widow

bears her covered pain deep inside

yet she smiles to every birth

Searching for the Man

I could not find a grain of pity

nor a pint of fraternity when…

when calamity felt upon Men

Those who mocked my good- doing

and those who laughed upon

my fear- now they are searching for serenity

in turmoil world where the Time braids

its epochs with the ashes and

the dust of civilizations

There's no Peace- stop pretending

the human benevolence when

none can scarify even a particle

of Goodness kept hidden

deep in their DNA

Not even a lump of smell kept

folded under the armpit

No feathers with tiny bells,

no praise songs for the kings,

no laments for the dead children

I still am…longing to meet a MAN

that is speechless yet he radiates beauty

and

splendor of heavenly bliss

in its divine reflection- if there ever

                was such…

he must have ascended

to the Love dimension of no return

It becomes felt

…on those moments

in those moments

far away from nowadays

on this moment

in this moment

far away from my Now-ness

there's a dew reflecting

my image

and

the spark of light

that opens the paths

of belief in

another time

in another place

that is closer

to the visible

that much close

it becomes invisible

it becomes felt

instead

The Morass

I am Wisdom in a transparent pot

and Imago on the top of the Metamorphosis

The water that decays across the time

a spoiled milk in brain's capillary

A window shall refresh the end

a storm shall throw all the frogs

on the ceiling of the old castles

From the river learn the current

the gold lumps it brings

       let they bloom

When the time comes

Gold hunters will come along

to saturate their lust

Protein war

Felt feathers of the fallen fallacy

a man who drunk from the test tube

a mind that is confused

in a crossroad of existence

Between today's richness and

tomorrow's hopeful abundance

Transformers of borrowed energy

The sky is vast within

Protein combination in

a cosmic walking creature

called the Body

The science shan't overpass morality

In order to fly,

a bird needs to fall

off feather wings and

fail for the balance

We need more love

and empathy

and wisdom

and…

Shall we abandon these?

we are doomed to be

replaced by machines

in seclusion

I stand firm

and

tranquil

not by my choice.

No!

I am here

I wait to reveal

who is human

and who

only resembles a human

For who knows

who conquered

the soul

and

who fly above…

darkly above

contaminated soil

 where mixed bog of blood

and

Bile created

little ponds

All over

The 25th hour of the day

The veil of past times failed and

the mask of deception faded

another boy laments the death of the Mother

before he mourns sharp claws of his ill-fate

that mercilessly chops his flesh- immature and

immaculate of sin.

He'll grow up when the winds of seasons

will blow and throw him from Nadir to Horizon

on the sea of life no compass may orient him toward

the Ocean of Love he never tasted the waters of.

Long plus time he'll embrace his stellar Souls

dispersed throughout ether and

find his solace at the 25th hour of the day

Image of our Winterreise

She brought the Christmas Stollen

few days after the New Year 2006

The days were still bitter

smell of war and spelt bread

evaporation stunned our stomach

On the land of spilled out blood

they told us…only poppies

break the monotony twang of golden- leaf fields

In our laments medley with the sound

of the barley leaves

metallic or crystalline echoes

nobody was able to discern

We took her to the cemetery

as miserable as sometime Turkish tombs

She started crying

braiding her memory-pain

with the vision of the child's death

She survived her holocaust

She never survived her suffer

She never survived her fear

Three Fives by Nine

I.

1. You said: "Be!" and it became six times

2. the repetition of foreign genetic code.

3. The red dice I throw in the Sea of Galilee.

4. I saw senile while drinking the last absolute of life.

5. Nard, Amber, Jasmine, Cedar, Horse skin.

6. I also made an elixir of aromas- to wait

7. thus that multiple wing light

8. to transport me to the below Arctic

9. and from there to the tears that I alone must smell

II

1. We tried to get drunk by dews and by drunkenness

2. our wine turned blood, until we got sick and

3. searching for the diluted ecstasy. We remained intoxicated

4. as those in love in the eyes of whom is visible only

5. the star distance, while cheeks are wet by tears and turn

6. to nacre. Here we are oh you Giants of Soul,

7. the God's servants. Not like us, not like anyone else, but like you

8. The white light while it enfolds you, while it covers

9. your rainbow color luminosity.

III.

1. I saw them crying and crying I felt

2. in suspicion shall I preserve this

3. stream of love for all

4. worlds in order to keep the freshness like

5. dew drops when they moisten a bending

6. grass-leaves. Doves observing and

7. butterflies with fluttering wings only

8. temporarily showing their beauty so to

9. leave their vestige like poets leaves their verses.

They call it Perfume

Seven thousand petals of the white rose

hundreds of tiny Maghrebian

Jasmine flowers

some Tonka bean and Civet

some Soul particles too

and Ormus to fixate

the splendor of the Life's joy

In my humility lays

a fractal of existence

In my humbleness- echo

of the dimension of the Grandeur

This Word penetrates deeply

tickling the hidden

and

dormant cells of loftiness

Whom to challenge

on the sky wide dome

clouds were forming the story

he tried to jump

never competing anyone

Himself was his own challenge

three times he competed

and exceeded himself-

himself was his insufficiency

himself was his counterpart

and

it remained so

The Lament of the Earth

How zeal fully you've preserved

the foreign narratives

you've adopted them

to sell them latter like a fog of all colors

Even today there are other-

sufficient to compete as who shall more and

who shall better keep the foreign past, and

there are others who strive to break

every membrane

to create new bio-algorithms

to uplift the life to another plane

to another dimension

Yet there will be Men

that will observe the World

here with the borrowed eyes

they will fold new images

in layers just like the fog thickens up

in this sky with a sole Sun

...and those who still want

to degust a fresh wine and

dry artisan cheese, petals of the May's roses

for a refreshment drink and a jam

When one day the exodus occurs

will Earth colonies remember the homeland

they left behind or they will only like a snake

that chucked its skin, never turn their head back

Go, experience the emptiness you've created, but

go aiming the return because

this Mother again shall await you open-armed

shall long for quite some time

accompanied with sounds of Cello, Santoor, Piano

and the chirping voices of the birds

with the wings of all rainbow colors

When in your recesses you hold your child

tell them that somebody here knew your repentance

tell them a bit about the greed that you took away

like the dowry which will fly above

the weight-less Souls of yours

and that you've measured everything

with the human scale

tell them about the Dice of Life and Death

...and the Death that defiled bearing heavy shadow

wearing black brocade gown spreading fear all over

tell them about the World with the two Suns and

with the pointing finger toward the Earth- toward Me,

this blue dew of Mercy that buries every evil in her chest

tell them about the stars you've counted

while in your fingers nipples appeared

tell them about the balloons of snivel from your noses

while playing the sweat drops leaked down the neck

tell them about wasps buzzing in your curly hair and

about the pond where swans were playing

while blue metallic color demoiselle mingled among cattails

tell them about Love you've tasted

but never succeeded to understand

tell

...about death for God's sake

the death of your most beloved and

the pain it caused

tell them at the end about the Separation and

 the wounds it incurred.

Go, try the emptiness you've created solely

but go with the aim of return because

this Mother shall again wait openheartedly

will long for some plus time

under the shade of wild Chestnut Tree

while bees collect the nectar

for some other life

An Emerald knoll

On an emerald knoll, I climbed

full of breath

full of self

Under the heavy-cold shadow

of an Ash-tree, I took

a rest for a while

a chrysoprase-epitaph

was observing me appallingly

crossly, and somberly, said:

"You, who in the world realized

that there is no East and there is no West

since your world is round.

You, who said:

so melt in Love

for eternity and a day more.

You, who discovered the secret in the light

while in grey nights, the Moon-walkers

prayed to God:

See that **Then-ness** *and this* **Now-ness**

are condensing with their naked bodies

in a solely single-being while you still

recall when Time was a God."

Evocation of beauteousness

Black is not a color

as I absorbs all beauty

> of the Universe

White is not a color too

as it erases all evil

by the brilliant shine of its face

soaked in all color

the Beauty emanates from

Talismanic Temple of Greatness

Glory be to the one who ascends

to the *Divine Loftiness*

With the kindlement of *His Light*

which today I summon

the *Possessor of the Greatest Light*

to ease and mild

the pain we all go through

…and the day shall come

dawn and dusk to have

a proper time- distance

From Him we sat

The hearing

The seeing

To hear the gurgling river

To see the falling colors from

                the rainbow

To collect the dews from

the wet grass leaves

To hear the metallic- gold sound

from the ripe wheat

To see the foam fruit pulps

chewed by the mouths

of the sweated foreheads of

hyperactive children

To hear the Dolphins

while copulating beneath

the big Sea

To see peptides arranging

deep in our chromosomes

To hear the flushing of electricity

in our Mitochondria

To cry while celebrating

the Humanity

Verily this is not a Poetry

verily I have condensed my soul

in the *Beauteousness of Certitude*

for this is indeed a pact

so…

make it appear!

quick !

quick !

make haste!

make haste !

right now!

right now!

…an union of Man with Men

an Union of Men with *The All*

what is visible,

semi-visible,

and

invisible

…an Union of Men with

heard, semi- heard and

un- heard

for He sees us all

for He hears us all

what we crave inside

and

what we display

as façade

for *He is The Hearing*

for *He is The Seeing*

Glory be to **The One**

The

One

O

N

E

How could I not fall in LOVE

It is us

who whiteness the evil

and

throughout millennia

we are told:

the World was bleeding

Yesterday

Today

and

Always

…but then the prophets were killed

and their most ardent proponents butchered

Today they chopped off the spirit

from the heart of the Poetry

and the Faith entirely rooted off from Literature

The body of morality became weakened

almost everything from the past

questioned

It seems we'll never learn

to live decently and how to

grow- not to compete with other

Intelligences but to at least

to cope with them and why not

fall in Love

Luminous alloys with no name

Shall one day biochemical algorithm

safeguard our worlds we do not

grow any expectation

The real wisdom lies in light

the secret is in there hidden

If the price of truth is in death

and the keys of prophecy gate

kept secret in tenfold boxes

made of brass and/ or other/ rather

luminous unnamed alloys

than all what remains to be discovered

in the future cycles of evolution

shall be visible as stripe

of slides and pulsating lasers

in a vast dark recesses of Unnamed

Dimensions that we are here, there, then,

now, previously, afterwards, all at once

manifested, manifesting manifestations

of Love that sees no color

Separate memory of the heart

What is a Poem for a God's sake

if it does not emanate from

the 40, 000 nerves of the heart

beamed directly to the bi-colored

brain substance that pulsates

Simultaneously

The waves of mystery down to the heart

his/her pure heart that

illuminates all cells

and tissues

all flash formations

and bones

and skeleton…

Talismanic devices for an AI age

we came down the valley

following the line

river descended from

the chest of the mountain

the sages left the talismanic devices

for the benefit of all

keeping that memory

in the eyes of the children

we saw the Divine presence

dews of the sweat in their forehead

testified our existence

in their ankle-bruises

we saw how

to undergo a pain

we heard zooming

of the wasps

in their curly hairs

oh so beautiful

this world shows

all its abundance

to live

and

to live

we remain

The wedding of Intelligencies

that was our last entanglement

in a wheat-field with heavy cobs

like the wise man walks modestly

in the same street he encounters

three times the same awed faces

we experience our double exposition

quantic is our love in essence

pain, sorrow, sobriety and spleen

all bridal like multicolor strings

upon our laugh all the difference

disappears- all heavy tears

are melted and leaked in

hot blushed cheeks. The wedding

of Intelligencies

occurred silently

the dowry was our breath and

our blood that turned crimson

serenity has it saying:

"Deeper the Silence

Shallower the Hearing"

I am still longing

(on Father's day)

Every day I was longing

for a rest in his lap

and for a kiss in my forehead

after reciting pre- sleeping prayers

Every now and then I long

what I missed in my childhood

I can just now realize he couldn't

no I couldn't

because

He took care about his orphan brother

A bit older than us

He couldn't make him missing

Missing even a cent

…a lap,

a moment of happiness

the emptiness

Grandpa left behind

Mom was always strong and

She remained so

Trough to the winds of life

She stood firm

Strong like faith

that holds the pillars of heaven

with the heart firmer than a diamond

She was

So many tears I saw in her face

yet so much love she gave

to us

to them

to everyone

to life

One day

When the sky re- acquires its bluneness

and the Ozone drops down the clouds

to wash our wounds

I shall wait men to deliver

their last sermon

or

a farwel speech

One day I may sing since

I know the song but my voice

fails to hit the last octave

despite that I shall continue

the chir will follow

and

neutralize my hissing and chirping

On that day we shall observe

mists of perfume forming

the beauty and pleasure

equal to none

On that day in the light

I shall dwell

Ignored sermon of the parrot

they started to count

tiny little hapinessess

assembling them as beads

in a silken thread for a rosary

to chant again an again

over and over- the names

the created themselves

it is as bricks are layered

in my biochemistry that

hinders the heavy

winds of time that blows

to ashes whatever apears

in a front of it and

blws away far beyond

the eyesight

they used to forget the malice

and all drakness it brought

forward and enfolded and

enveloped them tightly

squeezing their limbs and eyes

about to explode loosing

direction of observance.

There is a feast outside for

all man-like yet the Man

was humble reckoning

the development of this

manifestation looking

for the ernel of th elernel

there in light were mistey

is hidde

vision is blinded

and

mind is confused

...end

He was born in Rahovec, South East of Kosova, in 1972 and graduated at Prishtina University, Oriental Studies.

In the last thirty years he operated as Independent Scientific Researcher in the field of World Spiritual Heritage and Sacral Esthetics

Translated in English, French, German, Italian, Spanish, Polish, Greek, Serbian, Croatian, Bosnian, Macedonian, Bulgarian, Roma, Swedish, Turkish, Arabic, Hebrew, Romanian, Mongolian, Chinese, Maltese, Frisian, Sicilian, Bengali, Bahasa

Wrote many reviews, edited many books and anthologies, to mention: World Healing World Peace, Two volumes Anthology, Inner Child Press USA- 2014

Ambassador of Poets to Albania by Poetas del Mundo, Santiago de Chile

Director of Balkan Literature sector of the Kosovo PEN Center

Founder and member of South European Literature Association in Sofia, Bulgaria

Poet of the year 2014, Turkish Literary Magazine, IMZA, Yunus Emre Institute, Prishtina, Kosovo.

Award winning Poet Agim Ramadani, Stubëll- 2014.

Award winnig Poet, Naaji Naaman Prize for Poetry, Beirut, Lebanon, 2016

Member of Book and Publication Commitee- Ministry of Culture, Youth and Sport, (2012-2015).

Pulitzer Prize Nominated 2017

Doctor Honoris Causa, Universum Academy Lugano, Switzerland

Lifetime Academic Universum Academy, Lugano, Switzerland

Director of International Poetry Festival- "Poetry and Wine"- Rahovec, Kosovo

Founder of Fund for Cultural Education and Heritage in Kosovo

"The fragrances of the earth, the fragrances of the past, the fragrance of time that makes human sense... Fahredin Shehu inhales all the flavors of existence and does not write, no, but exhales the living eons of poetry! His poetry is the spiritualization of air, without which no life is possible! A bottle of Fahredin's age is filling, and miracles are just arriving. What do the winds of time do outside of sight?

The word of the Poet - sounds about this".

**Eldar Akhadov, Co-Chairman of the Literary Council
of the Assembly of Peoples of Eurasia, Member of the PEN International Writing Club,
Member of the Union of Writers of Russia, Ukraine and Azerbaijan**

This is poetry that seemingly rises like a mist emanating from ancient realms and mystical pathways. Fahredin composes like a bard of old, weaving verses as if they were musical passages.'
Ismail Butera, musician & storyteller, USA

Fahredin Shehu's poetry is elevating the Mundane into Spiritual realms. The words of his poems are akin to incantations, and he, the Poet, presents himself as an alchemist, creating poetic miracles and wonders from our Human experience.
Lena Ruth Stefanovic, PhD in Linguistics, Montenegro

There is an elegant clarity to the works of Fahredin Shehu... tactile, olfactory & ocular experiences which many of us seek to achieve in our work but few achieve. A careful, gentle voice in love with humanity / the planet and feeling for its wounds.

Les Wicks, Leading Australian poet & publisher

Fahredin Shehu. It is the intelligence of the senses, which is not purely intellectual intelligence, that guides and structures his poetry. Smell, in Proust, could evoke the past, the "temps perdu". In *Ormus* the senses also lead us to the past, to childhood, to the house, that immense world that lives on in memory. But they also take us further, because they update love, that love that leads to God. The smell of wet earth is the sensitive testimony of a paradise, an Eden that the poet reunions in the Unity that underlies all this magnificent set of poems.

Alfredo Fressia, Prof. of French letters, Poet and Literary critic, Uruguay/ Argentina

That is why Shehu's poems are meditative, soothing, and their perfume is discrete. The scent of jasmine comes from other times, not from our garden. Its melancholy is pleasant. The past has its own charm – the more scents, sounds, images, tastes and touches it contains, the more powerful it is. That is why it is a palimpsest. Memory turned into word, into verse, into poetry.

Katica Kulavkova, Academic, PhD in Comparative Literature-Sorbonne, Poet, Vice-President PEN Global, Skopje, Macedonia

Fahredin Shehu's poetry is a glorious Dionysian celebration, a fusion of the senses, revealing the cosmic beauty and giving birth to the Numinous. The reader wanders among colors, sounds and aromas mingled in time and space, combining memory and vision, the mythical and the contemporary. Thus, the golden essence of modern science encounters a "turquoise amphora" and impressions are recorded on an "epitaph of Graphene."

Miriam Neiger-Fleischmann, literary scholar (PhD), poet and painter, Jerusalem, Israel.

I want morebooks!

Buy your books fast and straightforward online - at one of world's fastest growing online book stores! Environmentally sound due to Print-on-Demand technologies.

Buy your books online at
www.morebooks.shop

Kaufen Sie Ihre Bücher schnell und unkompliziert online – auf einer der am schnellsten wachsenden Buchhandelsplattformen weltweit! Dank Print-On-Demand umwelt- und ressourcenschonend produziert.

Bücher schneller online kaufen
www.morebooks.shop

KS OmniScriptum Publishing
Brivibas gatve 197
LV-1039 Riga, Latvia
Telefax: +371 686 204 55

info@omniscriptum.com
www.omniscriptum.com

Printed by Books on Demand GmbH, Norderstedt / Germany